T0018379

Angela Gray's
Cookery School
Just Bread
Photographs Huw Jones

Angela Gray's

Cookery School

Just Bread

Photographs Huw Jones

GRAFFEG

Contents

Introduction

Prior to the first time I ever made bread, like many children growing up in the 60s and 70s, it came ready sliced in a plastic bag.

It was convenient and gave us everything from toast and a sandwich to fried bread and toasted soldiers. Little did I know that there was a whole world of bread out there just waiting to be discovered.

My adventure with making bread started in school. In the 70s we were so lucky to have been taught domestic science, where we learnt how to prepare and cook everything from rock cakes and jam buns to offal and fish; it really was amazing.

I remember baking bread for the first time using fresh yeast and the smell of it as we whisked it into tepid water with a little sugar, waiting for the froth to form. Then came the magic, mixing it into strong white bread flour to form a lovely stretchy dough, before kneading

it on a lightly floured surface until it tightened slightly and became smoother in appearance. I was hooked. I loved the physical process of mixing, kneading, knocking back and shaping all by hand, the aroma of the dough baking, watching it grow and turn golden and then, of course, there was the eating.

Since I forged my relationship with dough all of those years ago, I have travelled extensively with my work and sampled so many delicious breads along the way. If you think about the basic ingredients that go into making bread, they are very much the same the world over, yet the varieties are immense!

I have a very vivid memory of arriving in Paris to work as a private chef for a count and

countess. Apart from meeting the family and getting to know my way around their kitchen, I had to familiarise myself with the locality and where to shop for my ingredients. It was an education, full of wonder, discovering new ingredients and stunning displays of foods, all of which were inspirational.

The first time I walked into the local Boulangerie on the Boulevard Saint-Germain, I could not believe my eyes. Racks of beautiful hand-crafted artisan breads, croissants, pain au chocolat/aux raisin and, of course, bouquets of French baguettes in tall baskets. Naturally I wanted to buy one of everything, it was so difficult to choose! The flavour, texture and pure joy of eating those breads have stayed with me.

One country can have many regions with slightly different variations of a particular bread. Italian focaccia is a good example of this; there is the hard, almost biscuit-textured variety from Liguria; a flat Genoese style with deep finger-sized dimples, finished with olive oil and salt, then there's a similar thin, almost flatbread-like variety from Recco, used to make focaccia col formaggio (a cheese sandwich). In northern Italy there is a dolce/sweet variety which is eaten for breakfast and dipped into cappuccino, and so the list goes on.

The variety I have chosen for this book is focaccia al rosmarino, as it is more aerated than the aforementioned breads, with a lovely moist texture, and it is usually served with antipasto. We often make this in our Seasonal Italian classes and it always gets people giggling as they wrestle to tame the sticky dough. The finished bake is always received with gasps of delight, as if to say, 'How did that happen?'

My travels are very much reflected in my day-to-day work and the classes I teach give people a glimpse of a country's culture through a range of traditional dishes. Bread is always an integral part of a class and the process of making bread never fails to lift people's spirits. The recipes in this book have been enjoyed by our guests over the years and probably now form part of their own preparations at home when entertaining friends and family.

I always envisage people's reaction to the beautiful Catalan coca they have baked, a stunning bread to lay before people, with its rows of roasted vegetables, olives and cheese. It conveys such a warm welcome and a promise of great food to follow and it just makes me smile to think of it.

Another favourite is the Turkish flatbread lahmacun, which, like focaccia, has many variations throughout the Middle East. It is quite different from the common pizza we know, with its aromatic meaty topping finished with sumac. We sometimes serve this for lunch at our Middle Eastern Kitchen classes, with mild pickled chillies, labneh and salad with fragrant herbs. It is simple but beautiful food that captures that Middle Eastern culinary magic.

Each and every recipe in this book is like a close friend and holds many lovely memories spent with guests at the Cookery School, along with people I have cooked for over the years and my friends and family – bread unites us all.

To close, if I may share a little nugget of wisdom that I tell my guests in class every time we make bread: When you feel overwhelmed, unhappy, angry or at a loss, take to the kitchen and make bread. It has to be made by hand, so that way you can work through your emotions and as you knead the dough you will become much calmer. A little later, your efforts will yield something delicious and comforting, a reward for all the hard work you put into making it.

Such is life, and we must take time to enjoy it.

Angela x

Milk Loaf

Ingredients

500g strong white bread flour

7g sea salt

25g caster sugar

7g dried fast action yeast

30g unsalted butter

320ml whole milk

Makes 1 loaf

What you do

1 Make the dough

Put the flour in a large mixing bowl and mix in the salt, sugar and yeast.

2 Melt the butter in a small saucepan, remove from the heat and stir in 240ml of the milk and pop back on the heat until it is just warm to the touch.

3 Make a well in the centre of the flour and pour in the milk and butter (add the remaining milk to the pan and heat until just warm to the touch). Stir through the flour mix until the dough starts to form. As you stir, add enough of the remaining warm milk to form good, smooth dough – you may not need all of the milk.

4 Knead

Lightly oil your work surface and scrape the dough out onto it. Lightly oil your hands to prevent sticking and start to knead the dough, stretching it away from you and then rolling it back towards you. Repeat this process for 5-10 minutes until the dough strengthens and becomes smoother.

⑤ Rest
Lightly oil a large bowl and pop the dough inside, cover with a cloth or clingfilm and leave to double in size – this can take up to 2 hours depending on the temperature of your kitchen.

⑥ Knock back and prove
Lightly flour your work surface, tip the dough out and fold the edges into the centre. Fold in the ends to create a rectangle, flip it over and press down to degas. Lightly oil a 2lb/1kg loaf tin and tuck the edges and ends under to form a rectangle again, making sure it will fit into the tin nicely. Lift the dough into the tin, folds underneath, and make four shallow diagonal slashes with a sharp knife along the top. Place a sheet of oiled clingfilm over the top and leave somewhere warm to prove for about an hour until the dough just rises above the tin.

⑦ Bake
Preheat the oven to 220°C/200°C Fan/Gas 7. When the dough has risen, place in the centre of the oven and bake for 25 minutes. The bread should be risen, a lovely golden colour and sound hollow when tapped on the bottom. Remove the bread from the tin onto a wire rack and cool.

⑧ Serving suggestion
Thin slices, well buttered, are brilliant in a chip butty. It is also delicious toasted and topped with your favourite preserve.

I remember growing up in the '70s and loving a slice of Milk Roll spread with butter and jam. You can still buy it today off the shelf with its distinctive ridges, but a home-baked milk loaf is hard to beat. It is beautifully light in texture and has a lovely rich taste. For me, it's one step away from a brioche and is so good simply toasted and buttered.

Cottage Loaf

Ingredients

500g strong white bread flour

7g sea salt

1 teaspoon sugar

7g dried fast action yeast

50g butter, softened

300ml-350ml warm water

Sunflower oil for smearing

Makes 1 cottage loaf

What you do

1 Make the dough

Place the flour, salt and sugar in a large mixing bowl and mix. Stir in the yeast, then make a well in the centre and pour in three-quarters of the warm water and the soft butter.

2 Mix with a silicone spatula, adding a little more water as you go to bring the mixture to a nice soft, but not sticky dough.

3 Work the dough

Smear a little sunflower oil onto your work surface and scrape the dough onto it. Oil your hands and work the dough, stretching it away from you and then rolling it back towards you, repeating for about 5 minutes until the dough feels a lot tighter and springy to the touch.

4 Form the dough into a smooth ball and place on an oiled baking sheet or in an oiled bowl. Cover with clingfilm and leave in a warm, cosy place to rest until doubled in size.

5 Shape

When ready, tip out onto a lightly floured surface and fold the four edges into the centre. Flip the dough over and press down with your palms to expel any excess air. Cut away one-third of the dough and shape into a small ball, tucking the edges underneath. Give it a little twist to tighten and cup your hands around it to make a lovely small ball shape. Repeat this process with the larger piece of dough.

6 Sit the small dough ball directly on top of the large one, dip your first three fingers in flour and insert them through the top of the small dough ball, right through the larger one to the work surface. Repeat this a couple of times so that the two doughs become fused together.

7 Prove

Lightly dust a baking sheet with flour and place the assembled dough on top. Using a pair of scissors, make five snips around the top of the upper dough ball, then seven cuts around the lower dough ball. Slide the tray with the dough into a large plastic bag and leave for an hour or so until doubled in size and springy to the touch.

8 Bake

Set your oven to 230°C/Fan 210°C/ Gas 8, preheating for 15 minutes. To create a great crust, place a baking tin or dish, half-filled with water, in the bottom of the oven. Remove your risen dough from the bag, dust lightly with flour and place in the oven – at this point I generally spray the interior briefly with water and shut the door quickly. Bake for 20 minutes, then reduce the temperature to 190°C/Fan 170°C/ Gas 5 and continue baking for approximately 20 minutes.

Your cottage loaf should be well-risen, golden in colour and have a good crust. Test the interior doneness by holding the loaf in a thick cloth and tapping the base – it should sound hollow. Cool on a wire rack.

9 Serving suggestion

We love this with a hearty soup or a delicious ploughman's with a few of our favourite cheeses (it makes a great sandwich). Maybe an odd shape, but who cares?

This loaf is a bit of a rarity these days. Apparently, it was made in this way as a double-decker loaf so that more bread could be baked, taking up less room – genius! I remember making one at school and feeling a real sense of achievement, as it is notoriously tricky. If too heavy, the smaller top loaf can sink into the lower one during baking. The top can also pop off, but do not despair, this challenge makes it even more worthwhile!

Wholemeal Bread
Three Ways

This is a versatile bread and a firm favourite at home for breakfast. It toasts beautifully and has such a lovely wholesome flavour, enhanced by a greedy smearing of salted butter.

Ingredients

Wholemeal 1

400g strong wholemeal bread flour

100g strong white bread flour

7g dried fast action yeast

1½ teaspoons sea salt

50g butter (melted)

1 tablespoon light Muscovado sugar

300ml warm water

Wholemeal 2 – Seeded

75g mixed seeds – we use pumpkin, sunflower, flax and sesame

A little beaten egg and water

Wholemeal 3 – Malted

Replace the Muscovado sugar for malt extract

50g malt flakes or we used 50g Shreddies – they give a fabulous flavour and a fun finish to the loaf.

A little beaten egg and water

What you do

① Make the dough

Mix the flours, yeast and salt in a large bowl (if you are making the seeded recipe, add 50g of the seed mix to the dry ingredients – the remaining seeds will be used on the crust). If you are making the malted loaf, add 40g malt flakes or Shreddies (scrunched up) to the dry mix, keeping the remaining 10g of malt flakes/Shreddies for the top. If you are using Shreddies, leave them whole. Make a large well in the centre and add the melted butter, sugar and water. Mix these three ingredients together with a silicone spatula and then fold and mix through the dry ingredients to give a soft but firm dough.

② Knead

Lightly dust your work surface with flour and tip the dough out onto it. Knead for 10 minutes, stretching the dough away from you with one hand and rolling it back up towards

you with the other. Repeat this process for the time required, which will result in a firmer, smoother dough.

③ Rest

Lightly oil a mixing bowl and pop the dough in. Cover with a clean tea towel or use clingfilm and leave in a warm place until doubled in size. This can take up to 2 hours depending on the temperature of the room.

④ Shape

When the dough is ready, tip it out onto your work surface. Fold the edges into the centre, flip the dough over and gently press down with your palms to expel any excess air. Fold the dough into a rectangle, flip over again and tuck in everything neatly underneath. Pop into a lightly oiled and floured 900g loaf tin. Cover with a tea towel and leave to prove until doubled in size.

⑤ Finish your loaf

For a plain wholemeal loaf, simply sprinkle the top lightly with wholemeal flour.

⑥ For the seeded loaf, lightly brush the top with a little beaten egg and water, sprinkle the remaining seeds over the top and super gently pat them into place.

⑦ For the malted loaf, lightly brush the top with a little beaten egg and water and sprinkle with the remaining malt flakes or Shreddies.

⑧ Bake

Preheat your oven to 220°C/Fan 200°C/Gas 7 and place a baking tin or dish, half-filled with water, in the bottom of the oven.

⑨ Put your loaf in the oven, giving the interior a quick spray of water, and shut the door. Bake for approximately 30 minutes until risen, golden and firm to the touch. Test the base by tipping the loaf out carefully into a thick tea towel, and tap the base – it should sound hollow. If the bread is a little damp on the base, pop it back into the oven out of the tin, reduce the temperature to 200°C/Fan 180°C/Gas 6 and cook for a further 5 minutes.

10 Leave to cool on a wire rack.

 Serving Suggestion
Toast! Especially hot toasted and buttered soldiers for dipping into a rich egg yolk! Makes great sandwiches and perfect bread and jam for tea-time.

The recipes can also be used to make six gorgeous rolls, perfect for filling with goodies for lunch or a picnic. They only need 15-20 minutes to bake.

The addition of malt and seeds in recipes 2 and 3 just add more enjoyment to eating the end result.

BUTTER

Irish Soda Bread Three Ways

This non-yeast instant bread is so gratifying as it all happens so quickly with little effort. It goes well with most things, but freshly sliced and smeared with salty butter and then a spoon of fresh pan jam is hard to beat.

Ingredients

Soda Bread 1

250g plain white flour

250g plain wholemeal flour

100g porridge oats

1 teaspoon bicarbonate of soda

1 teaspoon sea salt

25g butter, cut into pieces

500ml buttermilk or natural plain yoghurt

To Finish – optional

Soda Bread 2 with a honey wash

50ml runny honey, 1 dessertspoon water, 1 dessertspoon rolled oats

Soda Bread 3 with mixed seeds

1 tablespoon mixed seeds and a little egg wash

What you do

① Preheat your oven to 200°C/ Fan 180°C/Gas 6 and dust a baking sheet with a little flour.

② **Make the dough**
Mix the flours, oats, bicarbonate of soda and salt in a large bowl. Add the pieces of butter and rub into the dried ingredients with your fingertips. Make a large well in the centre and pour in the buttermilk/ yoghurt. Using a spatula or dinner knife, combine the wet and dry ingredients together to form a good firm dough.

③ **Shape and finish**
Sprinkle a little flour onto your work surface and tip the dough out. Flour your hands gently and fold the edges to the centre, making quarter turns to form a smooth finish, then flip the dough over so the folds are underneath. Place the dough on your prepared baking sheet and gently flatten the top slightly – the

dough should be approximately 20cm in diameter. Cut a deep cross into the top, about three-quarters of the way through, as this will help the bread cook through and rise.

4 **For an Irish soda loaf**, simply sprinkle the top lightly with a little flour or oats.

5 **For the honey wash loaf**, the finish is applied after baking. Gently warm the honey and water together so it's easy to brush over the finished baked loaf, then sprinkle with the rolled oats and return to the oven for 4 minutes to toast the oats.

6 **For the seeded loaf**, lightly brush the top with a little beaten egg and water and sprinkle with the seeds.

7 **Bake**
Place in the oven and bake for 30 minutes. The loaf should be well-risen, deep golden in colour and dry to the touch in the centre. Tap the base to check that the inside is cooked through – it should sound hollow. If it doesn't, pop it back in the oven, upside-down, for a further 5 minutes.

8 Remove from the oven and slide onto a wire rack to cool.

9 **Serving suggestion**
Pan jam.

Fougasse

Ingredients

500g strong white bread flour

1 teaspoon fine sea salt

7g dried fast action yeast

2 tablespoons extra virgin olive oil

350ml hand hot water

Makes 1 fougasse

What you do

1 Place flour, salt and yeast in a bowl and stir through to combine. Make a well in the centre and pour in the olive oil and three-quarters of the water, mix briefly with a spatula, then fold through the dry ingredients, adding a little more water as needed to have a soft dough.

2 Lightly oil your work surface and tip the dough out, scraping any residue stuck to the bowl. Bring together into a ball and start the knead by stretching away from you with the heel of one hand, rolling it back up into a ball with the other and repeating. Carry on with this process for about 10 minutes – the dough should feel tighter and look smoother.

3 Place on an oiled baking sheet, smear the surface of the dough with olive oil and loosely cover with clingfilm. Leave in a warm place to rest until doubled in size.

This beautiful looking bread is shaped like an ear of wheat and can be found hanging up on hooks in the bakeries of Provence.

4 When the dough is ready, lightly flour your work surface, tip out the dough and fold the edges up to the centre and press down with your palms to expel any gas. Flip over and cut into two portions. Create an oval shape with your palms, pressing to increase the size and flatten, cupping your hands to neaten around the edges. It should be about 2.5cm thick. Alternatively use a floured rolling pin.

5 Place on two lightly floured baking sheets. Using a small sharp knife, cut two long slits right through the dough, 2.5cm/1" in from each end, down the centre of each dough, leaving about 7.5cm/3" between them. Then make six smaller slits angled slightly upwards to create an ears of wheat shape. I tend to stretch these cuts a little more once it has rested again. Dust the dough lightly with flour, cover with a clean cloth and leave to rise for 20 minutes – the dough will puff up nicely.

6 Preheat your oven to 220°C/Fan 200°C/Gas 7.

7 Bake for 15-20 minutes until crisp and golden. Remove and cool on a wire rack.

8 Flavours: you can add chopped herbs such as rosemary and thyme to the dough at the shaping stage. Chopped olives are also delicious.

9 **Serving suggestion**
Tapenade and a glass of Pastis on ice.

Like so many Mediterranean and European flatbreads, its origins are from ancient Rome, baked in the ashes of the hearth. It can be flavoured with herbs, chopped olives or just baked plain.

Pain de Campagne

Ingredients

Poolish

250ml hand hot water

160g white bread flour

30g wholemeal flour

½ teaspoon sugar

½ teaspoon dried fast action yeast

The dough

All the poolish

240ml hand hot water

480g white bread flour

½ teaspoon dried fast action yeast

1 teaspoon sugar

2 level teaspoons fine sea salt

Makes 1 loaf

This version of the bread is less laboured than some recipes and gives a great result.

What you do

1 Make the poolish

Ideally, make this the night before you plan to make your bread. I would suggest 12-16 hours for best flavour results. Mix together the water, flours, sugar and yeast in a medium bowl and cover with clingfilm. Leave on your work surface and let the magic begin. The next day the mixture will resemble a bubbly batter.

2 Make the dough

Pour the warm water into the poolish and mix together. Put three-quarters of the bread flour in a large bowl and add the yeast, sugar and salt. Pour in the poolish mix and combine. Leave to stand for 20 minutes for the flour to absorb the liquid (this will make the dough easier to handle).

3 Knead the dough

Tip the dough out onto your work surface and start kneading, adding the rest of the flour a tablespoon at a time until you have a smooth, soft dough. This will take approximately 10-12 minutes.

4 Proof 1

Lightly oil a mixing bowl and place the dough inside, smear the dough with a little oil and cover with clingfilm. Leave on your work surface to double in size – this will take about 2 hours depending on the temperature of your kitchen.

5 When the dough is ready, lightly flour your work surface and gently tip the dough out. Now it is time for kid gloves! It is important to handle the dough with care, maintaining as much of the aerated structure as possible, so fold each edge to the centre, turn the dough over and tuck the edges under to form a smooth, rounded shape – all of the folds should be underneath.

6 Proof 2

Lightly dust a baking sheet with flour and place the dough ball onto it. Oil a sheet of clingfilm and lay over the top. Leave for 1-1½ hours to proof. It should increase in size by half again in that time and will then be ready to bake.

7 Bake

Place a roasting tin or deep oven-proof dish in the bottom of your oven and fill with 300ml water. Heat the oven to the maximum temperature.

8 Remove the clingfilm from the risen dough, lightly dust with flour and make a slit in the top with a sharp knife. Place on the middle rack of the oven and turn the temperature down to 220°C/ Fan 200°C/Gas 7. After about 10 minutes, carefully remove the water vessel and bake for 25-30 minutes. Check if it is baked through by tapping it on the bottom – it should sound hollow. Cool on a wire rack.

⑨ Serving suggestion

Pain bagnat – salad, herbs, sliced
boiled egg, little tomatoes, pickled
red onion, olives, anchovies, tuna
and French dressing.

When I worked in the south of France,
I would sometimes spend a sultry
afternoon at the beach in St-Jean-
Cap-Ferrat, where the locals went.
My lunch would always be courtesy
of Phillipe who had a little tuck
van where he made and sold pain
bagnat – a hollowed-out loaf of pain de
campagne filled with layers of green
salad, tomatoes, anchovies and fresh
tuna in a zesty French dressing. It was
absolutely delicious and the perfect
feast for an afternoon by the sea.

Focaccia al Rosmarino

Ingredients

Biga

230g '00' flour

230ml water

¼ teaspoon dried fast action yeast

Final Dough

All the biga

200ml water

2g dried fast action yeast

350g '00' flour

70ml extra virgin olive oil

12g sea salt

To finish

3 tablespoons extra virgin olive oil

2 tablespoons water

2 sprigs fresh rosemary, fonds, roughly chopped

½ teaspoon salt flakes

Makes 1 large focaccia

What you do

1 Make your biga

Mix the flour, yeast and water together in a bowl, cover with clingfilm and leave to ferment for 12-16 hours. The biga should have doubled in size and look nice and bubbly on the surface.

2 Make the dough

Place all the dry ingredients in a large mixing bowl and combine. Make a well in the centre and scrape in the biga, add the 200ml of water, briefly mix and then incorporate the wet with the dry with a spatula to form a soft, loose dough. Work the dough in the bowl for 5 minutes with the spatula, drawing the dough upwards and over.

3 Lightly oil your work surface, transfer the dough onto it. Oil your hands and stretch the dough upwards and over away from you, like a circular motion. Repeat for 5 minutes until the dough becomes more elastic and smoother. Scrape the dough from your hands, wash them and then re-oil. Scrape the dough into your hands and, passing it from one to the other, smooth into a loose-formed dough and place on an oiled baking tray. Oil the surface of the dough and cover with clingfilm. Leave somewhere warm to rest until doubled in size – up to 2 hours. **Note:** I sometimes leave it in the fridge overnight for a slow rise, then take it out in the morning to fully rise.

4 Shape

The dough should be bubbly and sticky. Scrape the dough onto an oiled work surface and fold the edges into the centre to create a rectangular shape. Re-oil the baking sheet and flip the dough over onto it, pressing the dough from the centre outwards to fill the sheet. Brush the surface with a little olive oil and then cover with clingfilm, leaving to prove for about 30 minutes until puffed up.

There are many versions of this Italian classic. Some are eaten for breakfast dipped in coffee, others are used to make a simple but delicious sandwich. This recipe is for the bread we serve with a lovely antipasto.

5 Preheat the oven to 220°C/Fan 200°C/Gas 7 and place a baking tin or dish with about 100ml of water in it. Whisk together the olive oil and water and pour over the surface of the dough. Use your fingertips to make the holes that give the focaccia that classic look (if the dough is a little sticky, flour your fingertips before making the dimples). Sprinkle with sea salt flakes and sprinkle with the rosemary. Bake for 20-25 minutes until lightly golden. The crust will

be quite firm, but this will soften as it cools.

6 **Note:** If you have cake sandwich tins, you can line them with parchment cake liners and make round focaccia.

7 **Serving suggestion**
Serve warm with Italian charcuterie meats, olives, and roasted vegetables.

Finished with little characteristic dimples that soak up the olive oil, rosemary and sea salt topping, the dough has an excellent flavour with the addition of a pre-ferment called a 'biga'. This is easy to make, it just takes a little time, but the result is worth the wait.

Lahmacun

Ingredients

The dough

400g bread flour, plus extra to dust

3 tablespoons dried milk powder

2 teaspoons sea salt

3 teaspoons fast action dried yeast

2 teaspoons caster sugar

100ml olive oil

1 large egg

120ml lukewarm water

Extra olive oil to knead the dough/ oil the bowl

Topping

300g good-quality minced Welsh lamb

1 medium onion, finely chopped

1½ teaspoons sea salt

2 teaspoons ground cinnamon

2 teaspoons ground allspice

1 teaspoon red chilli flakes

5 stems flat-leaf parsley, leaves chopped

2 tablespoons pomegranate molasses

2 dessertspoons sumac

To assemble and serve

3-4 tablespoons tahini

30g pine nuts

2 tablespoons lemon juice

4 tablespoons Greek yoghurt

8 pickled chillies

Chopped parsley

Serves 4

What you do

1 First, make the dough – put the flour, milk powder, salt, yeast and sugar into a large mixing bowl and stir well to combine. Make a well in the centre and pour in the oil, break in the egg and mix both together briefly to combine. Pour in the water and mix through the dry ingredients to form a soft dough ball. If it is a little wet, add some flour to firm it up.

② Wash your hands and knead the dough lightly for about 5 minutes on an oiled surface to form a smooth ball. Place in an oiled bowl, brush the surface of the dough with olive oil, cover and leave in a warm place until doubled in size, about an hour.

③ **To make the topping** – put the beef, onion, sea salt, cinnamon, allspice, chilli, parsley, pomegranate molasses and sumac in a mixing bowl and mix thoroughly with your hands. Cover and place in the fridge until needed.

④ Divide the risen dough into two equal portions for large or eight portions for individual bases. Roll each into a thin base, dinner-plate-size for large, saucer-size for small. Brush each lightly with olive oil on both sides and place on the baking sheets. Cover and leave to rise slightly, about 15 minutes.

⑤ Preheat your oven to 210°C/Fan 190°C/Gas 7.

⑥ **To assemble** – divide the tahini between the bases, then divide the topping and spread it evenly. Finish with a scatter of pine nuts and a gentle squeeze of lemon juice.

⑦ Bake in the oven for 15 minutes; the crust should be lightly golden at the edges. Remove and finish the top with blobs of yoghurt, arrange a few pickled chillies and scatter some fresh chopped parsley. Serve with a lovely salad – I like to spoon a mound of it on top!

This is a delicious Turkish/Byzantine style flatbread topped with ground Welsh lamb. You can also use ground beef or keep it vegetarian using finely chopped vegetables such as onion, grated squash and aubergine.

Greek
Flatbread

Ingredients

400g strong white flour

8g dried fast action yeast

1 teaspoon sea salt

1 teaspoon sugar

2 tablespoons Greek olive oil

150ml Greek yoghurt, at room temperature

170ml warm water

To finish

Olive oil, for brushing and cooking

Dried Greek oregano (optional)

Makes 8

What you do

1 Make the dough

Combine the flour, yeast, sea salt and sugar in a large mixing bowl and make a well in the centre. Pour the olive oil, yoghurt and water into the well and briefly mix them together, then stir in the dry ingredients with a spatula to bring everything together to form a loose, non-sticky dough.

2 Knead

Scrape the dough onto a lightly oiled work surface and oil your hands. Work the dough into a ball and knead by stretching forward with one hand and rolling up back towards you, repeating for 5 minutes. The dough should feel tighter and springy. Put the dough in an oiled bowl and cover with clingfilm. Leave in a warm place until doubled in size, which can take from 45 minutes to 2 hours depending on the temperature of the room.

3 Shape

Turn the dough out onto a lightly floured work surface and divide into eight portions. Shape each portion into a ball, smoothing the edges and tucking them underneath. Flour a rolling pin and roll each dough ball out; making quarter turns every few rolls to make the circle even and form a 20cm round to the thickness of a £1 coin.

4 Cook

Heat a heavy-based pan and brush with olive oil. Prick each pitta all over with a fork. Lift a pitta into the hot pan and cook for approximately 3-4 minutes on each side. Lift the edge of the pitta once it puffs up and see if it is lightly golden underneath. Once it is, flip it over and complete the cooking. Remove and pop onto a plate. If you wish, you can brush lightly with a little olive oil and sprinkle with some Greek oregano – the flavour is exceptional.

5

Re-oil the pan and repeat the process until all the pittas are cooked. You can keep them warm in the oven set at the lowest temperature by covering the pittas with a piece of foil to prevent them drying out.

6

Use immediately, or pack together in a plastic bag to keep them moist.

7 Serving Suggestion

Classic tzatziki, hummus or a good Greek salad.

These flatbreads are so good and are simple to make. They are traditionally served with the Greek classic 'souvlaki', which we love and often make for a gathering.

It is very hands on, sociable food, eaten rolled up in paper. The breads are also delicious served with a simple mezze, particularly tzatziki, as the hot bread scooping up the cool yoghurt and cucumber is sublime!

Naan

Ingredients

300g strong white bread flour, plus extra to dust

1 teaspoon sea salt

7g dried fast action yeast

75g natural yoghurt

1 teaspoon runny honey

30g melted ghee or butter, plus extra to brush

150ml warm water

A little sunflower oil or ghee, for cooking

1 teaspoon nigella (black onion), sesame or poppy seeds (optional)

Makes 8

What you do

1 Put the flour and salt into a large mixing bowl and stir together, add the yeast and mix well.

2 Make a well in the centre and add the yoghurt, honey, melted ghee/butter and water, mix these together briefly, then stir into the dry mixture to form a smooth dough.

3 Lightly flour your work surface, tip out the dough and knead for about five minutes, stretching the dough away from you and then rolling back towards you. Repeat for the time required for a smooth dough.

4 Lightly oil a bowl, pop the dough in and cover with a dry, clean tea towel. Leave in a warm place to rest until doubled in size, about 90 minutes to 2 hours.

5 When the dough is ready, lightly flour your work surface and tip

out the dough. Fold the dough over onto itself and press down to expel the gas. Divide the dough into eight portions and shape each into a ball, bringing the edges to the centre then turning over and cupping with your hands to form the ball.

6 Flatten the dough balls and roll out into a flat circle that will fit into the pan – round or teardrop shape is fine. Brush the hot pan with oil or ghee and cook the naan one at a time. When the surface starts to bubble, flip over and cook the other side until a mottled brown finish appears.

7 To finish, brush with melted butter and sprinkle with nigella seeds, if using. Pop on to a baking sheet and keep warm, while you cook the rest of the breads.

8 To make ahead and store, pile the naan top of each other and seal in foil. Reheat at 160°C/140°C Fan/ Gas 3 for 10 minutes, remove the foil for 2 minutes and serve.

Paratha

Utterly delicious
with any curry
and chutneys.

Ingredients

425g plain flour, plus extra for rolling out

8g fine sea salt

30g sunflower oil

240ml warm water

To finish

224g softened ghee or butter

Flour, for sprinkling

Makes 8

What you do

1 Make the dough

In a large mixing bowl, combine together the flour and sea salt. Add the oil, mix through, then, using your fingertips, work into the flour. Make a well in the centre and pour in the water.

2 Using open fingers on one hand, mix the water and flour together. Lightly flour your work surface and scrape the dough out. Knead the dough, stretching it away from you then rolling it back up towards you, repeating for about 5 minutes until a smooth dough is formed.

3 Oil a baking sheet and pop the dough on. Smear the top with oil and loosely cover with clingfilm. Leave to rest for 1 hour, this will relax the dough and make it easier to roll out thinly.

4 After the dough has rested, divide into eight equal portions. Work with one portion of dough at a time, keeping the remaining dough covered with a damp towel or clingfilm.

5 First roll

Lightly flour your work surface. Form each portion into a ball, flatten and roll out as thinly as possible. The final dimensions of the dough should be roughly 16 inches by 10 inches, and should be paper thin and translucent.

6 Smear the surface of the dough with ghee/butter and sprinkle with a little flour. Starting at the edge furthest from you, roll the dough sheet up into a long, thin log shape. Coil each end inward until they meet at the centre, then fold the two coils onto each other and press together firmly, flattening slightly. Repeat with the remaining dough balls, place on two oiled baking sheets, smear with a little oil and cover with clingfilm; leave to rest again for an hour.

7 Form the paratha

Lightly flour your work surface, and roll each coil into an 8"/22cm round, rotating the dough after each roll so it stays in shape.

8 Cooking the parathas

The parathas are cooked twice, for the first cook, preheat a large heavy-based pan over a medium-low heat. Place a paratha in the pan, cooking for approximately 3 minutes on each side. Remove, then stack them one on top of the other. Preheat your oven to 120°C/100°C Fan/Gas 1 and place a baking sheet inside.

9 For the second cook, preheat the skillet again over a medium-high heat. Add 1 tablespoon of ghee, leave to melt and then add a paratha. Cook until golden brown and crispy, approximately 1 minute on each side. Once cooked through, scrunch up the paratha slightly to separate the layers; this will release any built-up steam and help to keep them crispy. Serve immediately or keep warm in a tea towel in the oven.

No Knead,
No Sweat

I have to say I was a little dubious when I first came across this, but it works! All your dough requires is a brief mix, an overnight stay of 12 hours in a warm place and some shaping up and proving the next day. The lengthy proving process gives this bread a delicious flavour, an excellent texture and crust, and it has that continental vibe about it.

Ingredients

500g white bread flour

3g dried fast action yeast

1¼ teaspoons sea salt

400-475ml warm water

Flour, for dusting

Makes 1 loaf

What you do

① Make the dough and rest

Put the flour, yeast and sea salt in a large bowl and give it a good mix with a silicone spatula. Make a well in the centre and pour in three-quarters of the warm water and mix through the dry ingredients, adding more water as required to give a good sticky dough (it should stretch as you pull up the spatula). Scrape the sides of the bowl, so that all the dough is together and cover with clingfilm. Leave it to rest on your work surface for 12 hours or leave it overnight somewhere warmish, around 21 °C, so it is ready to bake fresh in the morning.

② Shape

Flour your work surface and scrape your dough onto it, then flour your hands and fold each edge into the centre. Flip the dough over, then, cupping your hands, tuck the edges right under to create a ball shape. Sprinkle a square of baking parchment (large enough for the dough and to fit inside your Dutch oven/casserole pot), place the dough on it and sprinkle the top of the dough with a little flour and cover with a cloth. Leave for up to 2 hours to prove until nicely puffed up.

③ Re-Shape
Preheat your oven 240°C/Fan 220°C/Gas 9 and place a Dutch oven or heavy casserole pot with lid inside. (See my note for using a pizza stone.)

④ Use a pair of scissors to cut three slits across the top, or cut a cross in the centre with the tip of a sharp knife – this will help the steam escape and give the dough a good-looking crust.

⑤ Bake
Carefully take out your preheated Dutch oven or casserole, remove the lid and, using the edges of the paper, gently lift the dough into the pot. Cover with the lid and bake for

30 minutes, then remove the lid and bake for a further 25-30 minutes for a great golden crust finish. Lift the bread out of the pot using the paper and transfer to a wire rack to cool for at least 25 minutes before slicing.

⑥ **Note:** I have also baked this directly on a preheated pizza stone covered with a cast iron pot for 30 minutes, then a further 25-30 minutes without the pot. The results are excellent. You can also use a preheated heavy baking sheet and a Pyrex bowl over the top, a great tip I discovered on YouTube.

⑦ Serving suggestion
This bread is great with snacks, soup, toasted and topped with scrambled eggs, or pan-fried tomatoes.

Sourdough
Starter and
Sourdough
Bread

Sourdough
Starter

Sourdough Starter

Ingredients

700g strong white flour

Sourdough has become a baking phenomenon in recent years. Creating a good starter is essential to the taste and texture of the bread and achieving this is like a science project.

What you do

1 Mix together 100g of the flour with 125ml of warm water and beat together with a spatula until smooth and lump free.

2 Scrape into a 1L glass jar/container and cover with a damp tea towel for 1 hour. Next, seal the jar with a lid or seal the container with clingfilm, making sure it's secure. Find a nice warm home for it to ferment for the next 6 days.

3 You will need to feed your starter each day by scooping out half of the mixture (discard it), then adding in 100g of the flour and 125ml of warm water, stirring until combined.

4 Repeat this process daily, ideally at the same time – I do it before I go to bed.

5 As the days progress, you will begin to see bubbles on the surface and the aroma will be slightly acidic. These are good signs that your starter is developing nicely.

6 By the seventh day, your starter should be quite lively with bubbles and the aroma sweeter. The process is complete and ready to use.

It can become an obsessive pursuit in the quest to create perfection. A starter is a living thing and can be unpredictable depending on the ingredients, quantities and temperature used, so keeping the whole process simple is a good place to start.

The main thing to remember is that you are trying to achieve a strong starter by feeding it regularly at intervals to create yeast, and this will make better bread.

Sourdough Bread

Sourdough Bread

Ingredients

Levain

40g starter

20g white bread flour

20g rye flour

40ml warm water

For the loaf

All the levain (above)

400ml warm water

450g strong white flour

150g spelt or rye flour

15g fine sea salt

1 tablespoon light muscovado sugar

Sunflower oil, for your tin

Makes 1 loaf

What you do

1 Day 1 – Mix

First mix together all the ingredients for the levain in a large bowl. Cover with clingfilm or a clean tea towel and leave on your worktop overnight. The next day it will be nice and bubbly on the surface and ready to use.

2 Day 2 – Make the dough

Remove the clingfilm from the levian, pour in the warm water and mix together with open fingers, like a whisk. Add the flour and fold into the wet mixture, forming a loose, rough-looking dough. Cover with a clean, damp tea towel and leave for 1 hour.

3 Next, mix in the sea salt, wet your hands and mix through the dough thoroughly.

4 Stage 2

Now it's time to stretch the dough every 30 minutes over the next 2 hours. Use wet hands and insert them either side of the dough, gently stretch it up out of the bowl and flip it over onto itself. Repeat this five times, re-cover with the tea towel until the next time and so on. Towards the end of this stage the dough will be lighter, with more air bubbles.

5 Stage 3

Lightly flour your work surface and scrape the dough out. Using your scraper, fold the dough over onto itself, then repeat six times, adding a little more flour if the dough is sticking. You will feel the dough tightening as you do this and you will be able to achieve a better shape. You are aiming for a nice round shape.

This recipe uses a levain, made by mixing some sourdough starter, flour and water together. This will lessen the sourness of the starter, giving a better flavour to your loaf. I usually top up my starter at the same time here so that it keeps nice and lively.

6 Stage 4

Line a banneton basket with a linen cloth and liberally dust with flour, lift your dough into the banneton and lightly flour the top. Leave to rise until doubled in size – this can take up to 6 hours depending on the temperature of your kitchen.

7 Stage 5

When your dough is almost risen enough, set your oven to 240°C/220°C Fan/Gas 9. If you are using a pizza stone, place that in the oven to preheat now, if not, put a baking sheet to preheat. Place a baking tin on the base of the oven to preheat ready for the water that will create steam.

8 Sprinkle a baking sheet/stone with polenta, flip your risen dough out onto it and carefully peel away the cloth. Use a pair of scissors to cut five snips around the bread, one third of the way out from the centre, creating a circular pattern. Open the oven and slide the dough onto the stone/sheet and quickly add a cup of water to the baking tin.

9 Bake for 35-40 minutes until golden brown. Test if it's cooked through by turning it over and tapping the base – it should sound hollow. If it is not quite ready, pop it back in the oven for a few minutes.

10 Cool on a wire rack.

11 Serving suggestion

Top thickly with Welsh rarebit and grill.

Cornbread
with Chillies
and Cheese

Ingredients

125g butter, melted

1 small onion, finely chopped

125g corn cakes, processed to a powder

300g plain flour

1 tablespoon sugar

2 teaspoons baking powder

1½ teaspoons sea salt

150ml natural yoghurt

150ml whole milk

2 medium free-range eggs, beaten

1 medium red chilli, deseeded and finely chopped

125g extra mature cheddar, grated

Makes 1 cornbread,
serves 6-8

What you do

1 Put 1 tablespoon of the melted butter in a small pan over a low heat. Add the onion and leave to cook for 8-10 minutes until soft and lightly golden. Set aside to cool a little.

2 Tip all the dry ingredients into a large bowl. Stir together the yoghurt, milk and eggs and then mix with the dry ingredients until smooth.

3 Preheat the oven to 200°C/Fan 180°C/Gas 6.

4 Add the chilli to the mixture along with most of the cheese, the cooked onions and all the melted butter. Stir until well combined.

5 Spoon the mixture into a greased and lined 23cm (9in) cake or 1lb loaf tin and smooth over the surface with a spoon.

6 Cook in the preheated oven for 30-35 minutes until golden on top. Insert the point of a knife in the middle – it should come out clean when cooked through. Then, sprinkle over the leftover cheese and return to the oven for 5-10 minutes until golden and cooked through. Leave in the tin for a couple of minutes, then turn out, cut into triangles and serve warm.

During lockdown we couldn't source any polenta, so I came up with the idea of blitzing a load of corn cakes (like rice cakes but made of corn). They not only worked perfectly, but the flavour and texture was so much better! Now the secret's out. We love it toasted and topped with poached Burford Brown eggs and spicy tomatoes – yum!

Coca Bread

Coca bread is a
Catalonian flatbread.
I call this my welcome
bread; it sets the scene
for a relaxed and
enjoyable feast with
friends. It's also a
real favourite at the
Cookery School.

Ingredients

Dough

450g strong bread flour
5g sea salt
7g fast action yeast
1 flat teaspoon caster sugar
60g of extra virgin olive oil
300ml warm water

Topping

2 medium onions
2 sweet peppers
1 aubergine
8 cherry tomatoes
12 black grapes
100g Manchego cheese
12 green olives

Emulsion

4 tablespoons olive oil
1 tablespoon lemon juice
1 level teaspoon sweet smoked red paprika
1 fat clove garlic, grated
1 level teaspoon sea salt
1 rounded teaspoon chopped herbs
e.g. sage, rosemary or oregano

Serves 6-8

What you do

1 First, prepare the dough – in a large mixing bowl, mix together the flour, salt, fast action yeast and sugar. Make a well in the centre and pour in the olive oil and half of the warm water. Mix briefly with open fingers, then slowly add enough of the remaining water to form a smooth, elastic dough.
Note: You may need a little more water depending on the flour.

2 Pour a tablespoon of olive oil onto your work surface and spread it out with your hands to form a no-stick area. Pick up the dough and throw it forward onto the oiled surface still holding on to one end so it elongates out on the surface. Claw the dough backwards into a ball. Repeat this about 20 times until the dough firms up. Place in a lightly oiled bowl, cover and leave at room temperature until doubled in size.

3 Meanwhile, prepare the vegetables. Line two baking sheets

with foil or parchment paper. Peel and cut each of the onions into 8 wedges, place on the baking sheet and drizzle with a little olive oil. Roast the onions for about 30 minutes at 200°C/Fan 180°C/Gas 6 until soft.

④ Next, prepare the peppers, cut them in half, remove the stork, membrane and seeds and cut in half again. Add to the tray with the onions, drizzle with a little oil and return to the oven – the peppers need about 25 minutes. Now the aubergine: cut it in half lengthways and then into medium-sized half moons. Place on the second sheet, drizzle with olive oil and roast. Once the aubergines are in the oven, the vegetables should take about 20 minutes to finish cooking. **Note:** They need to be soft, not too brown. Cut the cherry tomatoes and grapes in half and cut the cheese into thin wedges.

⑤ Once the dough is ready, tip out onto the surface. Pick up the edges and bring them to the centre, creating a fold and pushing down at the centre, to create a large upside-down mushroom shape. Turn the dough over so the smooth side is facing you and use your palms to flatten it, pressing out any air bubbles.

⑥ Place on an oiled baking sheet and, starting from the centre, knuckle the dough outwards to fit the tin. Stretch out the corners then release back into the tin to get them to fit nicely.

⑦ Prepare the emulsion by mixing everything together. Pour over the dough and spread with a brush. Arrange the vegetables, fruit and cheese in panels along the dough, so that when you cut a strip across the bread you get a little of everything. Finish with the olives and a little drizzle of olive oil.

⑧ Bake at 220°C/Fan 200°C/Gas 7 until crisp and golden – this should take around 25 minutes. If the dough is a little soft in the middle, reduce the temperature to 180°C/Fan 160°C/Gas 5 and cover with foil and cook for a further 10 minutes.

Levant
Man'oushe
and Za'atar

Ingredients

400g strong white bread flour

1 teaspoon fine sea salt

1 teaspoon sugar

5g dried fast action yeast

250ml hand hot water

1½ tablespoons extra virgin olive oil

Topping

125ml extra virgin olive oil

3 tablespoons za'atar (see recipe on page 115)

Makes 6

Bread is an integral part of daily meals and this one is typical of a pan-cooked flatbread. It is topped with a signature topping of za'atar and olive oil, which tastes divine!

What you do

1 Put the flour, salt, sugar and yeast in a large mixing bowl and stir through to combine. Make a well in the centre and pour in 200ml of the water and the olive oil, mix briefly, then stir through to combine the dry ingredients. Add a little more water as needed to form a nice soft dough.

2 Lightly oil your work surface and scrape the dough out. Oil your hands and work the dough into a ball, then knead for 5 minutes, stretching the dough away from you then rolling it back up towards you. Repeat the process until the dough is smooth and shiny.

3 Oil a baking sheet, pop the dough onto it, smear the surface with a little oil and lay a sheet of clingfilm over the top. Leave somewhere warm for 1½-2 hours to double in size.

4 When the dough is ready, tip it out onto a lightly floured surface and divide into 6 portions. Flour your hands and pick up each portion of dough and form into a ball by smoothing the surface over with your thumbs, whilst turning it with your fingers. Place on your work surface and, using a floured rolling pin, roll each ball out to form a mini round flat bread, popping any air bubbles as you go.

5 Mix together the olive oil and za'atar. Cut a couple of sheets of baking parchment and line two baking sheets, put a rolled dough on each and sprinkle both with 2 teaspoons of the za'atar mixture, leaving a border around the edge. Set aside for 5 minutes (prepare them in a relay as they won't all fit in a domestic oven at the same time).

6 Bake at 220°C/Fan 200°C/Gas 7 for 8-10 minutes until golden at the edges.

7 Once baked, cool on a wire rack, but serve warm with toppings of your choice.

8 **Serving suggestion**
Little bowls of fresh sliced vegetables; tomatoes; labneh, pickled chillies.

Middle Eastern cuisine has become really popular in the last decade or so with the likes of Ottolenghi, Sarit Packer and Itamar Srulovich, Claudia Roden and Anissa Helou opening the door to a wonderful aromatic mix of herbs, spices and ingredients that have fuelled our love for this food.

Za'atar

Ingredients

1 tablespoon dried thyme

1 tablespoon cumin seeds

1 tablespoon coriander seeds

1 tablespoon toasted sesame seeds

1 tablespoon sumac

½ teaspoon sea salt

¼ teaspoon chilli flakes

What you do

1 Heat a small frying pan and add the cumin and coriander seeds. Stir and dry-roast for 1 minute.

2 Remove and tip into a mortar and pestle and add the sesame seeds, sumac, sea salt, chilli flakes and thyme.

3 Crush together with the pestle for a couple of minutes. Should you have any leftover, store in an airtight jar.

Rugbrød – Danish Rye Bread

I once met the great Danish food activist Claus Meyer at an event ahead of an amazing talk he gave. He shared how he and some of his fellow like-minded Scandinavian chefs collaborated on a mission to re-work traditional recipes and bring them back into restaurants. United, they successfully rebooted Scandi cuisine, making great, seasonal food more accessible to all.

I have never heard anyone speak so passionately about bread, the one food that unites so many people and cultures. So, this recipe is inspired by Claus Meyer, and we absolutely love this bread. It has goodness, comfort and deliciousness all in one loaf.

Ingredients

Soaker Grain and Seed Mix

500g cracked rye kernels

200g flax seed/linseeds

200g sunflower seeds

100g pumpkin seeds

1L cold water

Dough

800g rye flour

7g dried fast action yeast

600ml cold water

50g sea salt

80g molasses/black treacle

Butter for your bread tin

Makes 3 small loaves

What you do

1 Day 1 – Make the soaker

I make the soaker in advance to give it 24 hours to soak/ferment. Take a large mixing bowl, put all the soaker ingredients in and mix. Cover with clingfilm and leave on your work surface for 24 hours.

2 Make the dough

Combine the flour and yeast in a large bowl and mix well. Make a well in the centre, pour in the water, salt and treacle. Whisk these together briefly before stirring through the dry ingredients to form a dough. Cover with clingfilm and leave on your work surface for 24 hours to develop.

3 Day 2

Combine the soaker with the dough, turn out onto a lightly floured work surface and knead for 10 minutes. Note that the dough will not stretch like white or wholemeal dough, due to the lack of gluten. Fold the edges to the centre and press down, repeating this action for 10 minutes.

4 Divide the dough into three portions and butter or oil three bread tins that can each hold approximately 2 litres. Shape each portion of dough into a rectangle, folding the edges to the centre and the ends over to form the shape. Flip over and neaten with the edges of your hands. Pop them into the prepared tins and cover with clingfilm or a damp tea towel and leave to prove until the dough has risen to the top edge of the tins. This can take up to 3 hours depending on the temperature of your kitchen.

5 Preheat your oven to 180°C/160°C Fan/Gas 4 and bake the bread for approximately 1 hour 20 minutes. The bread should be only slightly raised, dark brown in colour and firm to the touch.

6 Remove the breads from the tins and cool on a wire rack.

7 Wrap the cooled bread in foil or clingfilm. It is better left for 24 hours before eating and will keep nicely for up to 10 days in an airtight container.

8 Serving suggestion
Danish open sandwiches or toasted for breakfast with butter and honey.

German
Rye Bread

German breads are delicious and varied, from light, milky milchbrötchen to super dark, dense pumpernickel. They are generally very healthy breads containing whole grains.

Ingredients

600g rye flour

100g strong white bread flour

½ teaspoon caraway seeds

½ teaspoon fennel seeds

½ teaspoon ground anise

½ teaspoon ground coriander seeds

7g dried fast action yeast

2 level teaspoons sea salt

1 tablespoon sunflower oil

450-470ml warm water

1 tablespoon cider vinegar

Makes 1 loaf or 2 smaller loaves

What you do

1 In a large bowl, add the rye and white bread flour, stir in the yeast and salt, followed by the caraway, fennel, ground anise and coriander seeds and mix together. Make a well in the centre, pour in the oil, three-quarters of the water and the vinegar, mix briefly, then gradually mix into the dry ingredients, adding enough additional water to form a smooth dough ball.

2 Lightly flour your work surface and turn the dough out. Work the dough, folding and pressing repeatedly for 5 minutes. Form into a ball, place in an oiled bowl and cover with a cloth. Leave in a warm place to rest until doubled in size.

3 When the dough is ready, turn out onto your work surface, flatten with your palms and fold the edges in, then flip it over and cup your hands around the dough to shape into a nice ball shape. Flatten the top slightly and cut a shallow cross into the top with the tip of a sharp knife.

4 Place on a baking sheet lined with parchment paper, cover with a cloth and leave for 30-40 minutes to prove – it should have puffed up nicely and be ready to bake.

5 Preheat the oven to 200°C/ 180°C Fan/Gas 6. Place a shallow tin or casserole dish on the base of the oven and pour in 600ml of warm water; I also use a water spray.

6 When the dough is ready to bake, pop it in the oven and reduce the heat to 180°C/160°C Fan/Gas 4, quickly spray the interior with water, close the door and bake for 20 minutes.

7 Next, carefully remove the dish/ tin of water from the base of the oven, allow any excess steam to escape, then close the door and bake for a further 40-45 minutes until the crust has a nice medium to dark finish.

8 Remove from the oven and tap the base to check if cooked through – it should sound hollow. Cool on a wire rack.

The recipe I have chosen is a typical rustic German bread which has a lovely aromatic, nutty taste. It has quite a heavy texture and is perfect served with hearty soups.

Danish Cinnamon Rolls

When I lived in London, there was a fabulous bakery on a small street outside Cannon Street train station and, if I wasn't running late for work, I would pop in and buy a few cinnamon rolls to share with my fellow cooks. The rolls were always warm and deliciously fragrant having just been baked; a great way to start the day with a good cup of coffee.

Ingredients

Dough

150ml whole milk

2¼ teaspoons dried fast action yeast

1 large free-range egg

1 egg yolk

50g caster sugar

½ teaspoon vanilla extract

½ teaspoon ground cardamom

½ teaspoon fine sea salt

375g white bread flour

60g unsalted butter, softened

1 egg for egg wash

Filling

125g unsalted or salted butter, softened

160g light, soft brown sugar

1½ teaspoons ground cinnamon

Pinch of salt (if using salted butter, don't add this)

Topping

100g icing sugar

1 teaspoon vanilla paste

2-3 tablespoons milk

Makes 8

What you do

1 Make the dough

Pour the milk into a pan and gently heat until hand hot. Put the egg, egg yolk, sugar, vanilla extract, cardamom and salt in a large bowl and mix briefly. Whisk in the warm milk and the yeast. Slowly stir in the flour, using a wooden spoon until the dough starts to form; at this stage start to add the softened butter a teaspoon at a time until incorporated.

2 Lightly flour your work-surface and scrape the dough out. Knead for 7-10 minutes until firmer and smooth. Your finished dough should be neither sticky, nor too dry. Place your dough in a lightly oiled bowl, cover with a cloth and leave somewhere warm to double in size – this can take up to 2 hours.

3 Make the filling
Put the softened butter, brown sugar, cinnamon and salt in a bowl and mix together to form a smooth paste.

4 Shape and bake
Once the dough is ready, lightly flour your work surface and, using a rolling pin, roll the dough into a rectangle that is about a ¼ inch/0.5cm thick.

5 Spread the filling evenly over the top and roll it up from the shorter edge into a nice fat log. Cut the log into 1½ inch/3cm-thick slices. Place them on two parchment-lined baking sheets. Cover them with a clean cloth and leave until doubled in size again, approximately 30 minutes.

6 Preheat your oven to 200°C/Fan 180°C/Gas 6.

7 Whisk together an egg with a little water and brush evenly over the surface of the buns. Pop into the oven and bake for 15-17 minutes until puffed and deliciously golden; they will smell amazing!

8 Remove from the oven and lift the buns onto a cooling rack. Mix together the icing sugar, vanilla and milk and drizzle over the buns from the end of a teaspoon.

9 Serving suggestion
A good cup of coffee, chai or rooibos tea, or, if you're feeling really indulgent, a hot chocolate.

Bara Brith

Bara brith translates as 'speckled bread' and is sometimes baked without yeast, using self-raising flour to give it a lift. The bread has a lovely rich fruity flavour and is delicious served with a cheeseboard.

Ingredients

The dough

400g strong white bread flour

100g wholemeal or rye flour

75g butter, softened, plus a little extra for your tin

7g fine sea salt

65g light brown sugar

7g dried fast action yeast

1 teaspoon dried mixed spice

300g dried mixed fruit – I love currants, raisins and sultanas

1 teaspoon orange zest, grated

1 medium free-range egg

225-275ml well-brewed lukewarm tea

To finish

1 tablespoon runny honey

Salted butter, to serve

Makes 1 large loaf

What you do

1 Put both flours into a large bowl, dot in the butter and rub with your fingertips until the mixture resembles fine breadcrumbs. Add the sea salt, sugar, yeast and mixed spice and stir through. Stir in the dried fruit and orange zest, coating the fruit with the dried ingredients.

2 Make a big well in the centre, add the egg and tea, beat them together briefly, then fold into the dry mixture to form a dough.

3 Lightly dust your work surface, tip the dough out and work it by stretching it away from you, then rolling it back towards you. Continue for 5 minutes, or until the dough is smooth.

4 Lightly butter a bowl and place the dough inside, cover with clingfilm or a clean tea towel and leave somewhere warm until doubled in size. This can take

up to 2 hours depending on the temperature of the room.

5 When the dough is ready, tip it out onto your work surface and bring the edges into the centre. Flip over and press down to expel the excess gas 'knock back'. Fold into a rectangle that will fit into a 900g/2lb loaf tin. Butter the tin and place the shaped dough inside with the folds underneath. Cover again and leave to prove for 30 minutes; the dough should be nicely puffed up.

6 Preheat the oven to 200°C/ 180°C Fan/Gas 6. When the loaf has risen, place it in the oven and bake for approximately 20 minutes. The loaf should be well risen and a lovely golden colour.

7 Tip the loaf out of the mould and tap the base – it should sound hollow, indicating it is cooked through. Put the loaf on a cooling rack, gently warm the honey in a small pan and brush over the top of the loaf. Leave to cool.

The ingredients

Strong bread flour – this contains a high level of gluten, a protein that will give your dough great elasticity and stretch, along with a beautiful chewy crust when baked. There are many flours on the market these days, including the ancient grain spelt, several rye flours, white and unbleached, along with various wholegrain varieties.

Yeast – is a very clever little fungus that is the main leavening ingredient used in most breads. When added to flour and water, it gobbles up starch, which in turn produces carbon dioxide; this fills up any air bubbles, giving the bread its light, airy texture.

Salt – is, of course, needed to add flavour to bread. More importantly, it controls the rate of yeast fermentation and strengthens the gluten network, giving your dough a better shape and colour.

Water – the importance of this ingredient in breadmaking is so underestimated. It allows everything to happen, including the formation of gluten dissolves the salt, sugar (if used) and yeast and helps to disperse it through the dough. It also determines the consistency of the bread. If you compare a slice of white farmhouse with a slice of focaccia, it is clear to see the difference. The more aerated, bubbly texture in focaccia is due to the wetness of the dough, whereas the farmhouse is a more closed, uniform crumb as a result of using less water.

Oil/fat – oil or fat is sometimes added to improve texture, to give a softer crumb, a great crust and good flavour.

Sugar – adding a little sugar simply feeds the yeast and speeds up the rise during proofing. It does affect texture in baking generally, especially sweet bakes such as cakes and muffins etc. Sugar locks in moisture, giving a softer result to the mixture when baked, so a little in bread can help with the final crumb.

Poolish – is a pre-ferment made 12-16 hours in advance, then added to a dough. It gives bread good flavour, a lighter texture and an aerated appearance when sliced.

Biga – like poolish, this is a pre-ferment used in Italian baking, giving breads such as ciabatta their distinct open, airy texture and a great crust.

Levain – also known as a sourdough starter, levain is another pre-ferment. However, this one is kept alive by regular feeding. It is rich in natural wild yeasts and bacteria (lactobacilli) and used to replace the role of commercial yeast in sourdough breadmaking. It also gives the bread its flavour and results in a good chewy crust.

Making a basic dough

Making bread dough is very simple, you just need a nice big mixing bowl, some digital scales and a spatula or dough scraper for mixing – or just use your hands!

A basic bread has just four ingredients: strong bread flour, salt, yeast and water. Most dough recipes start the same way.

- Weigh the flour and tip into a large mixing bowl.

- If using dried fast action yeast, mix this directly into the flour. If you are using fresh yeast, double the weight of dried is generally required, crumbled into the flour and rubbed in with your fingertips, like making a crumble.

- Add the salt and mix through (add sugar here if using in your recipe).

- Make a big well in the centre of the dried ingredients, pour 90% of the water in and fold through the flour using a dough scraper/ spatula or your hand.
  Note: I always hold back a little water; some flours are greedier than others, so you may or may not need it all, or you may need a tablespoon or two more to achieve your dough. Take note of what your recipe says – some doughs are wetter than others, some sit overnight to ferment etc.

- Once the dough is formed, follow the next stage of your recipe.

Kneading

This is a little workout, but it can be fun and a little obsessive. I usually put the radio on and set my timer for 10 minutes.

Lightly flour or oil your work surface (some recipes use oil rather than flour). Scrape the dough out and start to work/knead it. Firmer doughs can be stretched using the heel of your hand. Put your body-weight behind the heel of your hand and lean forward, pushing the dough away from you, stretching it out, then rolling or folding it back towards you. Press down and repeat. This can take 5-10 minutes. You will feel the dough tightening as you work the gluten, and if you stretch out a piece of the dough between your middle and index finger and thumb, it should look smooth and not grainy.

Note: A wetter dough like focaccia may need the help of a dough scraper to get through the kneading process. Stay with it, and don't be tempted to add more flour!

Resting

Take a mixing bowl or a baking sheet and lightly oil it, pop your lovely dough in, smear a little oil over the surface and cover with clingfilm or a clean tea towel. Now the wait; you are looking for the dough to have doubled in size. The rising process can take anything from one to three hours depending on the temperature, the moisture level in the dough and gluten formation. Some of you may have a dough proving setting on your oven, which will definitely help speed things up.

Check if it's ready

The best test for dough readiness is to give it a gentle poke with your fingertip. If the dough springs back up immediately, then leave it a little longer as it still has some growing to do. However, if your finger leaves a mark, then there is no more stretch left, so it's time to move to the next

stage. **Note:** Don't leave it too long, otherwise the structure will start to soften as the air bubbles deflate.

Degas/knock back and shape

Decant your risen dough onto a lightly floured work surface. Fold in the edges and press down with your palms. This will flatten or degas the bubbles that have formed. Shape it according to your recipe and then bubbles can reform in the proofing or second rise stage. At this point the formed dough is placed into a tin or on a baking sheet depending on the bread you are making. The dough is covered again until it has risen to its full potential as before, however, it doesn't take as long this time, about 30 minutes to an hour (heavier rye doughs may take longer).

Note: I sometimes leave my dough for the second rise in the fridge overnight. The slow proofing process gives the bread a deeper flavour. You will need to bring the dough to room temperature the next day before baking; just shape the finished dough ready to go in the oven and leave it to rise fully.

Baking

Always preheat your oven to the maximum temperature for at least 20 minutes. I often use a pizza stone, Dutch oven or cast iron pot for some breads and these are also preheated. The introduction of steam can help the dough rise and form a lovely crust, so I pop an ovenproof dish on the base of the oven and pour in about 300ml of hot water. Once the bread has risen and starts to colour, the water bath can be carefully removed so the crust crisps up nicely. To check if your bread is cooked through, you need to tip it out into a tea towel and tap the base – it should sound hollow.

Making bread can bring you such a sense of achievement. When you look at the ingredients you start with and what you end up with, it really is quite magical.

About Angela Gray

Angela opened the doors to her Cookery School at Llanerch Vineyard in April 2010. She is now in her twelfth successful year and has already been voted into the Top 10 UK Cookery Schools by *The Independent* and *The Telegraph*. Her Cookery School has also been shortlisted for the Best Cookery School in the Great British Food Awards and chosen to join an elite

selection of 50 top schools in The National Cookery School Guide. Angela has created a wide variety of cookery classes and events, where she loves to share her knowledge, skills and anecdotes.

Angela has worked prolifically in the food world, starting her career as a personal chef working in Europe and North America. Her clients have included an esteemed list, from European aristocracy to high-profile clients such as Lord Lloyd Webber. Angela then moved into the restaurant business, where she developed her relaxed style of cuisine with a strong Mediterranean influence.

She later returned home to Wales, where her culinary path changed direction and led her back to school. After three years at university, she graduated with a BSc Honours degree in Food Science. Whilst studying, Angela also ran a small fine-dining catering business and held a twice-monthly Cooking Club in her home. The Club lasted for 15 years and was to form the basis of the television cookery series that was to come her way.

Angela was talent-spotted after producer Mark John (Vision Thing) read some of her articles in a magazine. Next came two prime-time cookery series for BBC Wales, *Hot Stuff* and *More Hot Stuff*, with Angela as the presenter and chef. She also has several radio series to her credit, including *My Life on a Plate* and *Packed Lunch*. Angela remains a consistent contributor in the media world.

Together with her team, she has entertained people from all over the world and created a popular venue and experience for corporate team building and private events. She is also a mentor to young budding culinary talent and is most at home when sharing her passion for great cooking. In her own words, 'it's a dream job!'

A seven-book project with Graffeg began in 2016, a series of seasonally themed cookery books, *Winter Recipes, Summer Recipes, Autumn Recipes* and *Spring Recipes*, along with *Festive Recipes, Delicious Bundles* and the latest, *Just Breads.* Angela has drawn her inspiration from the seasons, her career in food and her childhood food memories to help craft the pages.

All seven books have now been published and each recipe vibrantly captured by food specialist and photographer Huw Jones, enough to inspire anyone's culinary creativity. The books offer something for all palettes and preferences, so find the perfect dish to enjoy and share with family or friends through the seasons with Angela Gray!

Dedication

To all the people I have taught, baked for and shared bread with over the years – it has brought us all together.

People we love

- Bacheldre Watermill Stoneground Flours, available on Amazon

- Shipton Mill
www.shipton-mill.com

- Castle Dairies – the best butter in the world! – www.castledairies.co.uk

- Halen Mon Sea Salt
www.halenmon.com

Metric and imperial equivalents

Weights	Solid
15g	½oz
25g	1oz
40g	1½oz
50g	1¾oz
75g	2¾oz
100g	3½oz
125g	4½oz
150g	5½oz
175g	6oz
200g	7oz
250g	9oz
300g	10½oz
400g	14oz
500g	1lb 2oz
1kg	2lb 4oz
1.5kg	3lb 5oz
2kg	4lb 8oz
3kg	6lb 8oz

Volume	Liquid
15ml	½ floz
30ml	1 floz
50ml	2 floz
100ml	3½ floz
125ml	4 floz
150ml	5 floz (¼ pint)
200ml	7 floz
250ml	9 floz
300ml	10 floz (½ pint)
400ml	14 floz
450ml	16 floz
500ml	18 floz
600ml	1 pint (20 floz)
1 litre	1¾ pints
1.2 litre	2 pints
1.5 litre	2¾ pints
2 litres	3½ pints
3 litres	5¼ pints

Other Angela's Cookbooks

Angela's cookbooks bring together a collection of recipes inspired by the seasons, her childhood, travels and career in food. They also form the basis of many of the courses run at her Cookery School.

Winter Recipes

Everything naturally warms up in colour and flavour in this recipe collection. Angela uses a wide range of ingredients to invigorate the palate, from aromatic spice blends to the punchy flavours of pomegranate molasses, porcini and truffle.

Spring Recipes

Expect fresh, zesty flavours, vibrant colours and lots of inspiring ways to enhance your day-to-day cooking at home.

Summer Recipes

A rich collection of recipes from Angela's travels and her time spent working in the South of France. Barbecuing, dining al fresco, entertaining friends, it's all here.

Autumn Recipes

Colours and flavours become richer and deeper in this book and recipes embrace the wonderful harvest of seasonal ingredients. Angela shares easy ways to entertain so you can be the host with the most.

Festive Recipes

A very special collection of recipes from the 'Festive Kitchen' event, where Angela demonstrates a range of inspirational recipes that are all showstoppers, guaranteed to 'wow' friends and family throughout the Christmas and New Year celebrations.

Delicious Bundles

Recipe ideas inspired from a global melting pot of classic dishes that combine to make memorable meals with family and friends.

Just Bread
Angela Gray's Cookery School
Published in Great Britain in 2022 by
Graffeg Limited.

Written by Angela Gray copyright © 2022.
Photography by Huw Jones copyright
© 2022. Food styling by Angela Gray.
Prop styling and post production by Matt
Braham. Hand modelling by Caitlin Owen.
Designed and produced by Graffeg Limited
copyright © 2022.

Graffeg Limited, 24 Stradey Park Business
Centre, Mwrwg Road, Llangennech,
Llanelli, Carmarthenshire, SA14 8YP,
Wales, UK. Tel: 01554 824000.
www.graffeg.com.

Printed in China

ISBN 9781802580839

1 2 3 4 5 6 7 8 9